# The copywriting community reacts to
## *Instant Inspiration for Copywriters*

**David Garfinkel**, author, *Breakthrough Copywriting*

> "I would urge everyone who writes copy to get this book. Some of the quotes are stunning — stuff you've never heard, and they'll expand your mind. But the reason I think you need to get it is all the reminders, from top names in the business, of what sometimes you forget to do that costs you money."

**Drayton Bird**, author, *Commonsense Direct & Digital Marketing*

> "Einstein said, 'Example isn't another way to teach; it is the only way to teach.' Yet depressingly few copywriters study what the best writers said about writing. Here is pithy, wise advice not just from people I knew – Gene Schwartz, David Ogilvy, Joe Sugarman, for instance – but from good writers of all kinds. Nathaniel Hawthorne, Elmore Leonard, Jeanette Winterson, Maya Angelou, Ernest Hemingway, John Steinbeck …This is your short-cut to better writing. Not just copywriting: ANY writing."

**Tom Albrighton**, author, *Copywriting Made Simple*:

> "Scott has created an absorbing collection of tips, ideas and opinions about every aspect of copywriting. You'll find time-honored wisdom from David Ogilvy and Rosser Reeves, alongside insights from today's master practitioners like Joanna Wiebe and Ann Handley. Dip into it whenever you need a helping hand or a new direction – it won't let you down."

**Steve Slaunwhite**, author, *The Everything Guide To Writing Copy*

> "There are only a few copywriting books I would consider to be 'keepers'. This is one of them. What makes this book great is it gives you an instant dose of inspiration whenever needed. And we copywriters tend to nｅ…"

Instant Inspiration for Copywriters
R. Scott Frothingham

Published by FastForward Publishing

ISBN: 9798635318164

# INSTANT INSPIRATION
## FOR COPYWRITERS

R. Scott Frothingham

with a forward by
**Robert W. Bly**
author of The Copywriter's Handbook

# Don't read this book.

It wasn't designed to be read from cover to cover. It was put together to be used as a tool.

You're a copywriter. Sometimes you need a word of inspiration or a quick piece of advice from an expert at your chosen craft. Pick up this book, flip through a few pages, and get some encouragement or a tip from David Ogilvy or Seth Godin or Gary Halbert or Ann Handley or Eugene Schwartz or Ernest Hemingway or Dan Kennedy or … I could go on, but you get the idea.

 Right now, at your fingertips you have over 500 observations directed specifically to you, a copywriter. So, when you could use a little input from highly accomplished writers, randomly select a page or two and focus on a couple of the quotes. Think about those morsels of wisdom. Use them to inspire you, to fuel your passion, and to guide your copywriting.

Then go back to work.

As copywriters, our story always ends with: Then go back to work.

Keep this collection of insights and advice* handy so when you need a nudge from a master, it's right there for you. And don't hold back, you can check out one a day and not repeat for well over a year.

*Scott*

R. Scott Frothingham

I'm a copywriter and the author of this book in which I only used other people's words. Which has me thinking I should find a better word than author. Compiler? Assembler? Collector? Arranger? Curator? Anthologist? Accumulator? It's deadline and I'm going with *author*. When you're a copywriter, you are never really finished, you keep fine-tuning until you hit the deadline and submit it. Then you go back to work.

> PS If someone gave you this book, thank them. If you bought it for yourself, pat yourself on the back for making a wise decision. If you are considering buying it, don't delay; complete the purchase it right now so you can put it to immediate use enhancing your career.

*I could have said "compendium of sagacity" instead of "collection of insights and advice" but I followed the guidance of David Ogilvy on page 23.

This book will make you a better copywriter. Buy it now.

# Foreward
By Robert W. Bly, copywriter

*Instant Inspiration for Copywriters* may be the only "instant results" book I've ever read that delivers what is promised in the title: practical, real-world tips and advice – more than 500 pearls of wisdom in all -- that both inspires and teaches you to write the strongest copy you can.

Specifically, here's what I think it gives you in a refreshingly quick, plain-speaking, and experienced-based copywriting guide:

• *Motivation.* When you read advice from so many contributors who love writing so much that they cannot contain their enthusiasm, the enthusiasm becomes infectious and is usefully passed on to you, the reader. This can't help but lift you out of the doldrums and give you renewed energy to go back to the keyboard and write with engagement and gusto.

• *Techniques.* Many of the ideas and tips shared can, when you follow them, actually make you a better copywriter capable of producing stronger copy on every assignment you tackle. By putting these battle-tested copywriting axioms to work, you will increase readership, response, leads, and conversions from your ads, emails, and other promotions.

• *Reality checks.* Sometimes we think our problems in copywriting and business are unique – that they plague us and no one else – which can get us down. In this book, you'll see your problems as a copywriter are not unique to you. You'll discover that they affect many other copywriters, and more important, learn how these copywriters solve, get through, or get around these common problems – and how you can, too.

• *Wisdom.* The combined experience of the many copywriters quoted this book can be measured not just in years or decades, but in centuries. Yes, many of these copywriters are smart. Many are copywriting masters. These centuries of accumulated experience deliver to you a breadth and depth of wisdom unmatched by any other copywriting book available today.

• *Sharing.* Perhaps more than any other professionals, writers are eager, open, and willing to share what they know with other writers—including colleagues and competitors. Again, I know of no other copywriting book that shares this much knowledge from so many skilled practitioners so freely.

I know I will return to this book again and again for inspiration, ideas, knowledge, tips, and wisdom. And I will become a better copywriter each time I do.

Now you can dive into *Instant Inspiration for Copywriters* and come along with me for a lifetime of learning, improving, writing stronger copy, and becoming a more successful copywriter with each passing year.

If it sounds like writing, I rewrite it. Or, if proper usage gets in the way, it may have to go. I can't allow what we learned in English composition to disrupt the sound and rhythm of the narrative. – Elmore Leonard

When I write an advertisement, I don't want you to tell me that you find it "creative." I want you to find it so interesting that you buy the product. – David Ogilvy

Your job is not to write copy. Your job is to know your visitors, customers and prospects so well, you understand the situation they're in right now, where they'd like to be, and exactly how your solution can and will get them to their ideal self. – Joanna Wiebe

Writing: the profession in which you stare at a computer screen, stare out the window, type a few words, then curse repeatedly. – Drew Goodman

Nobody reads ads. People read what interests them. Sometimes it's an ad. – Howard Gossage

Tools are great, but content marketing success is about the wizard, not the wand. – Jay Baer

You either have to write or you shouldn't be writing. – Joss Whedon

The brands that can connect with clients in a real way will win. – Gary Vaynerchuk

Metaphors are a great language tool, because they explain the unknown in terms of the known. – Anne Lamott

Making a decision to write was a lot like deciding to jump into a frozen lake. – Maya Angelou

We have become so accustomed to hearing everyone claim that his product is the best in the world, or the cheapest, that we take all such statements with a grain of salt. – Robert Collier

Every product has a unique personality and it is your job to find it. – Joseph Sugarman

Convince yourself that you are working in clay, not marble, on paper not eternal bronze: Let that first sentence be as stupid as it wishes. – Jacques Barzun

People will do anything for those who encourage their dreams, justify their failures, allay their fears, confirm their suspicions, and help them throw rocks at their enemies. – Blair Warren

Here's the only thing you're selling, no matter what business you're in and what you ship: you're selling your prospects a better version of themselves. – Joanna Wiebe

The secret of all effective advertising is not the creation of new and tricky words and pictures, but one of putting familiar words and pictures into new relationships. – Leo Burnett

Instead of representing the buyer's expectations, needs, wants, and concerns, many personas are built around a profile of what the business would like its ideal buyer to be. – Jennifer Havice

The very first thing I tell my new students on the first day of a workshop is that good writing is about telling the truth. – Anne Lamott

It has long been my belief that a lot of money can be made by making offers to people who are at an emotional turning point in their lives. – Gary Halbert

There is your audience. There is the language. There are the words that they use. – Eugene Schwartz

Comfort the afflicted. And afflict the comfortable. – Carl Ally

*Arrogance undermines quality.*
*Great copywriters know when their own ideas stink and treat them accordingly.*

Brad Shorr

The best marketing – and the best copy – is not about duping the reader into believing something, but about amplifying their need, alleviating their fear and exciting them to action. – Joel Klettke

Brevity doesn't mean bare bones or stripped down. Take as long as you need to tell the story. – Ann Handley

There is a secret every professional artist knows that the amateurs don't: being original is overrated. The most creative minds in the world are not especially creative; they're just better at rearrangement. – Jeff Goins

And what is wrong with playing with words? Words love to be played with, just like children or kittens do! – David Almond

Effective copywriting is salesmanship in print, not clever wordsmithing. The more self-effacing and invisible your selling skill, the more effective you are. Copywriters who show off their skills are as ineffective as fishermen who reveal the hook. – Gary Bencivenga

It's not the fear of writing that blocks people, it's the fear of not writing well; something quite different. – Scott Berkun

I hate writing, I love having written. – Dorothy Parker

Connect with the reader by adding personality into the content. Be weird or funny or ironic or deep and thoughtful, but be yourself! Your readers are people and value authenticity. – Cristina Garcia

I've learned that any fool can write a bad ad, but that it takes a real genius to keep his hands off a good one. – Leo Burnett

Writing is like making love. Don't worry about the orgasm, just concentrate on the process. – Isabel Allende

Every piece of copy is a conversation. – Scott Frothingham

Tap a single overwhelming desire existing in the hearts of thousands of people who are actively seeking to satisfy it at this very moment. – Eugene Schwartz

Writer's block simply means the structure for an idea is broken. If you give ideas a robust structure, then writer's block vanishes forever. – Thomas Clifford

The web is not a murder mystery. Tell them who did it in the first sentence. – Gerry McGovern

Speak how you feel and write how you speak. – Glenn Fisher

I realized a great truth about headlines: Your level of interest is directly proportional to the presence of two factors: benefit and curiosity. – Gary Bencivenga

What I am doing here is taking the reader by the hand and leading him exactly where I want him to go. It seems like a small point and, maybe it is, but is the little touches like this that keeps the letter flowing, the reader moving along, and, it relieves him of the burden of trying to figure out what he is supposed to do when he finishes reading a particular page. – Gary Halbert

People don't like to be sold, but they love to buy. – Jeffrey Gitomer

Learn a lesson from successful weight loss marketing. They talk about their customers before they helped them lose weight. They ask questions that bring out similar stories about their prospect's current situation. Only then do they show the BEFORE and AFTER pictures, letting the prospect imagine themselves as the AFTER. – Scott Frothingham

People aren't interested in you. They're interested in themselves. – Dale Carnegie

*Easy reading is damn hard writing.*

Nathaniel Hawthorne

Writing is hard work. A clear sentence is no accident. Very few sentences come out right the first time, or even the third time. Remember this in moments of despair. If you find that writing is hard, it's because it is hard. – William Zinsser

Good advertising is written from one person to another. When it is aimed at millions it rarely moves anyone. – Fairfax Cone

If dogs don't like your dog food, the packaging doesn't matter. – Stephen Denny

In writing good advertising it is necessary to put a mood into words and to transfer that mood to the reader. – Helen Woodward

No passion in the world is equal to the passion to alter someone else's draft. – H. G. Wells

What matters isn't storytelling. What matters is telling a true story well. – Ann Handley

Writer's block? I've heard of this. This is when a writer cannot write, yes? Then that person isn't a writer anymore. I'm sorry, but the job is getting up in the fucking morning and writing for a living. – Warren Ellis

Since your single goal is to make the sale, treat your copy like a salesperson and evaluate it on performance. – Demian Farnworth

Copywriting with passion, creating a shared, emotional experience of desire, delight, excitement, and awe, is the primary challenge all copywriters face. – Aaron Orendorff

If you tell your prospect how bad things are in a way they can identify with and relate to, then they know that you know the way it really is because that is the way it really is for them. – David Garfinkel

The greatest thing you have working for you is not the photo you take or the picture you paint; it's the imagination of the consumer. They have no budget, they have no time limit, and if you can get into that space, your ad can run all day. – Don Draper

The answer to why people share content is quite simple. It all comes down to social currency. Basically, people share when it makes them look good. – Neil Patel

It takes a big idea to attract the attention of consumers and get them to buy your product. Unless your advertising contains a big idea, it will pass like a ship in the night. I doubt if more than one campaign in a hundred contains a big idea. – David Ogilvy

The mind thinks in pictures, you know. One good illustration is worth a thousand words. But one clear picture built up in the reader's mind by your words is worth a thousand drawings, for the reader colors that picture with his own imagination, which is more potent than all the brushes of all the world's artists. – Robert Collier

Marketers have a tendency to try to abstract their messages to the point that everything can be said in two to six commonly used words, which somehow gives us the comforting sense that we've created a polished marketing message. As if that's the goal. Let me leave you with this: polish doesn't convert. – Joanna Wiebe

If you don't know why your reader should care, then you can't help them see why they should care. – Scott Frothingham

The good news is that YOU – as an email copywriter – will NOT have to do boatloads of research for your client in order to write stunning, money-drenching emails. You simply have to be able to relax and write a good story. – Matt Furey

You must make the product interesting, not just make the ad different. And that's what too many of the copywriters in the U.S. today don't yet understand. – Rosser Reeves

The reason it seems that price is all your customers care about is that you haven't given them anything else to care about. – Seth Godin

*Revision means throwing out the boring crap and making what's left sound natural.*

Laurie Halse Anderson

Keep the message simple, emotionally engaging and relatable. People want a connection, whether it's humor or something more serious, and they're more likely to share it with others. – Jeff Fleischman

The most powerful element in advertising is the truth. – William Bernbach

The product that will not sell without advertising will not sell profitably with advertising. – Albert Lasker

The mental faculties used for brainstorming/planning are wildly different from those used for writing. Give each the proper time to work. – Brett Snyder

Advertising, an art, is constantly besieged and compromised by logicians and technocrats, the scientists of our profession who wildly miss the main point about everything we do…" – George Lois

You sell on emotion, but you justify a purchase with logic. – Joseph Sugarman

No sentence can be effective if it contains facts alone. It must also contain emotion, image, logic, and promise. – Eugene Schwartz

The time to begin writing an article is when you have finished it to your satisfaction. By that time you begin to clearly and logically perceive what it is that you really want to say. – Mark Twain

Nobody counts the number of ads you run; they just remember the impression you make. – William Bernbach

We are busy, easily distracted, and short on time, our noses buried in our cell phones. Before you can get someone to visit your store, check out your website, or learn about your great product or idea, you have to convince them you have a story they should listen to. – Matthew Luhn

The best advertising should make you nervous about what you're not buying. – Mary Wells Lawrence

If your readers don't make it past the first few sentences, they sure as hell ain't making it to your call to action. – Hassan Ud-deen

If you can't turn yourself into your customer, you probably shouldn't be in the ad writing business at all. – Leo Burnett

The copywriter is a translator, a bridge. Our job is to make the familiar unusual and to make the unusual familiar. – Jim Punkre

You should write because you love the shape of stories and sentences and the creation of different words on a page. Writing comes from reading, and reading is the finest teacher of how to write. –Annie Proulx

When you are looking directly to your swipe file for inspiration, don't look for phrases to copy, or formulas to fill-in-the-blanks. Think about the psychology behind the copy. – Casey Meehan

A click-worthy title is actually worth a lot more than just a perfectly keyword-targeted title. – Rand Fishkin

If you can't reduce your argument to a few crisp words and phrases, there's something wrong with your argument. – Maurice Saatchi

Grab your visitor's attention via engaging content, inspire them to trust you, and then convert them into buyers. – Scott Frothingham

Never stop testing, and your advertising will never stop improving. – David Ogilvy

No one cares about you, they care about themselves. – Neville Medhora

*Make it simple.*
*Make it memorable.*
*Make it inviting*
*to look at.*
*Make it*
*fun to read.*

Leo Burnett

The thing all writers do best is find ways to avoid writing. – Alan Dean Foster

Any copywriter should be a good enough writer to string a decent sentence together, then stack those sentences up for dramatic narrative flow. Understanding where your prospect's head is when they arrive at your copy… entering their conversation, and then taking it over? That's the bigger challenge. – Kevin Rogers

All the elements in an advertisement are primarily designed to do one thing and one thing only: get you to read the first sentence of the copy. – Joseph Sugarman

Writer's block is a fancy term made up by whiners so they can have an excuse to drink alcohol. – Steve Martin

Focus less on "selling" with copy and more on engaging. Marketing copy, especially taglines, shouldn't be about what you want to get across, but rather about delighting the reader. – Amanda Hinski

If your content isn't driving conversation, you're doing it wrong. – Dan Roth

Copy is a direct conversation with the consumer. – Shirley Polykoff

Today's buyers want to feel like an audience of one. – Lee Rowley

In an online world, our online words are our emissaries; they tell the world who we are. – Ann Handley

Our business is infested with idiots who try to impress by using pretentious jargon. – David Ogilvy

Edit fiercely, judging your copy by its ability to generate the desired response, not its length. – Scott Frothingham

Talk to someone about themselves and they'll listen for hours. – Dale Carnegie

The key ingredient to a better content experience is relevance. – Jason Miller

Sell people what they want to buy. – Gary Halbert

Breakthrough Advertising is not about building better mousetraps. It is, however, about building larger mice – and then building a terrifying fear of them in your customers. – Eugene Schwartz

*A writer is someone for whom writing is more difficult than it is for other people.*

Thomas Mann

Today it's important to be present, be relevant and add value. – Nick Besbeas

There's no such thing as "hard sell" and "soft sell." There's only "smart sell" and "stupid sell." – Leo Burnett

The road to hell is paved with adverbs. – Stephen King

Your readers should be so compelled to read your copy that they cannot stop reading until they read all of it as if sliding down a slippery slide. – Joseph Sugarman

Creating good chatbot copy is an art designed to create a participatory adventure for the subscriber. – Mary Kathryn Johnson

Writing is easy. All you do is stare at a blank sheet of paper until drops of blood form on your forehead. – Gene Fowler

The best copywriters are the most tenacious researchers. Like miners, they dig, drill, dynamite, and chip until they have carloads of valuable ore. John Caples advised me once to gather seven times more interesting information than I could possibly use... Research is the infallible cure for writer's block. – Gary Bencivenga

An ad is finished only when you no longer can find a single element to remove. – Robert Fleege

When we talk about something negative, it doesn't have to be dramatic, but there should be some cost of turning your offer down. What's yours? – Amy Harrison

Whether it's B2B or B2C, I believe passionately that good marketing essentials are the same. We are all emotional beings looking for relevance, context, and connection. – Beth Comstock

Your email intro and body are the setup, and your call to action is the punchline. If your setup is poor, your response will be poor. – Kelvin Dorsey

I have always believed that writing advertisements is the second most profitable form of writing. The first, of course, is ransom notes. – Philip Dusenberry

Even when you are marketing to your entire audience or customer base, you are still simply speaking to a single human at any given time – Ann Handley

By limiting access to something, you also increase people's desire for it. – Dan Lok

Nobody has the time or patience to read linear content. Instead of writing long indigestible blocks of text, make your content skimmable. – Tania Cheema

Advertising is salesmanship mass produced. No one would bother to use advertising if he could talk to all his prospects face–to–face. But he can't. – Morris Hite

Kindly remember that the obvious is always overlooked. – Drayton Bird

It's none of their business that you have to learn to write. Let them think you were born that way. – Ernest Hemingway

Thinking that every idea and piece of content you create must be the first of its kind is a trap. – Sujan Patel

Every purposeless line in a message robs the receiver of their most valuable asset - their time. – Derek Doepker

Marketing is not a battle of products. It is a battle of perceptions. – Jack Trout

If the average person needs a dictionary to translate your copy, you've lost multiple sales already. – Martina Mercer

Buy me and you will overcome the anxieties I have just reminded you of. – Michael Schudson

You need to woo your audience. You want them to trust you, and you do that by posting relevant content that speaks to them, about them, and for them. – Rachel Miller

Personality is a point of differentiation no one can copy. – Yaro Starak

Now, for those of you who stubbornly continue to write nonprofit emails (i.e., emails that put subscribers to sleep, have dog puke sales copy, and have resistible offers), I have one thing to say to you: Stop it! – Kelvin Dorsey

Do not make the mistake of holding your idea close to your chest… Submit it to the criticism of the judicious. – James Webb Young

The more vivid the picture the words paint in your mind when you read them, the greater the readership, the greater the response. – Michel Fortin

*Conversion copy narrows the focus to a single goal. The goal is to get people to act.*

Kate Toon

So, before you begin the writing, be sure you know the purpose or mission or objective of every piece of content that you write. What are you trying to achieve? What information, exactly, are you trying to communicate? And why should your audience care? – Ann Handley

Panicky despair is an underrated element of writing. – Dave Barry

The real advertising writer who is after results makes the reader want something – and then provides what the reader will consider a good excuse for buying it. – Clyde Bedell

Begin your bullets with dynamic action words, and keep them brief and punchy. – Casey Demchak

Facts are irrelevant. What matters is what the consumer believes. – Seth Godin

Almost all good writing begins with terrible first efforts. You need to start somewhere. – Anne Lamott

Writing isn't about using big words to impress. It's about using simple words in an impressive way. – Sierra Bailey

Every single copywriter who ever made a bundle of money for their clients, and made a name for themselves in the process, always saw things from their market's point of view. 100% of the time. Every... single... damn... word... of their copy was written with one single objective: to resonate with the reader. – Kelvin Dorsey

We need to be a fan of our own work. – Joe Gill

We are all apprentices in a craft where no one ever becomes a master. – Ernest Hemingway

Any writer can spew out 1,000 words on a given topic. A great writer condenses the topic down to 300 powerful ones. – Brad Shorr

Always be open to ideas. No matter when they appear. No matter where they come from. No matter how strange they might seem. – Glenn Fisher

Find the inherent drama in your product. – Leo Burnett

People think copywriters are obsessed with words. This isn't correct. The word should be "infatuated" – it fits the context better. – Jamie Thomson

Don't be afraid to let your personality show through in your content. It makes it more relatable and entertaining. – Michael Brenner

You write an ad to make money. You're not writing your ad just to write an ad. – Matt Furey

Copywriting is so much more than just text. Nowadays copywriters need to understand UX concepts, design, and SEO. The more complementary skills you can add to your arsenal, the more effective your writing will become. – Neville Medhora

A cautious creative is an oxymoron. - George Lois

Soon is not as good as now. – Seth Godin

Effective content marketing is about mastering the art of storytelling. Facts tell, but stories sell. – Bryan Eisenberg

The best headlines are those that appeal to the reader's self–interest, that is, headlines based on reader benefits. They offer readers something they want – and get from you. – John Caples

*A limited offer has unlimited appeal.*

Dan Lok

Writing is like sausage making in my view; you'll all be happier in the end if you just eat the final product without knowing what's gone into it. – George R.R. Martin

Fear and self-doubt are the deadly enemies of creativity. Don't invite either into your mind. – Don Roff

Where a web page is the terrain, the copywriter's the tour guide, instructor, concierge, maître d', and of course, sales clerk. If the copy can't seal the deal, it must offer something compelling to start some sort of relationship. – Barry Feldman

The greatest mistake marketers make is trying to create demand. – Eugene Schwartz

It's not about trying to crank everything you can into the article. It's about delivering value and persuading people that you can solve their problem in as few words as possible. – Tim Soulo

I think we could say that the creativity of an idea works in inverse proportion to the amount of time available and the number of people involved. – Howard Gossage

The vast majority of products are sold because of the need for love, the fear of shame, the pride of achievement, the drive for recognition, the yearning to feel important, the urge to look attractive, the lust for power, the longing for romance, the need to feel secure, the terror of facing the unknown, the lifelong hunger for self–esteem and so on. Emotions are the fire of human motivation, the combustible force that secretly drives most decisions to buy. When your marketing harnesses those forces correctly you will generate explosive increases in response. – Gary Bencivenga

Proofread carefully to see if you any words out. – William Safire

We are all storytellers. We all live in a network of stories. There isn't a stronger connection between people than storytelling. – Jimmy Neil Smith

The copywriter uses words as tools to persuade and motivate an audience. You persuade your readers that you have something valuable to offer; you motivate them to acquire it for themselves. This is the essence of effective copywriting. – Richard Bayan

If you don't actually care about the words, don't expect your customers to either. – Scott Frothingham

Being a writer is a very peculiar sort of a job: it's always you versus a blank sheet of paper (or a blank screen) and quite often the blank piece of paper wins. – Neil Gaiman

Make your advertising too valuable to throw away. – Sonia Simone

If you're trying to make a point ... just make it! Some writers write like they're prepping a debate team, trying to preempt opposing arguments and using super technical jargon. There is no debate team. There's just your reader, who wants you to get to the point clearly and directly. – Neville Medhora

Always enter the conversation already occurring in the customer's mind. – Dan Kennedy

I try to leave out the parts that people skip. – Elmore Leonard

We want consumers to say, "That's a hell of a product" instead of "That's a hell of an ad." – Leo Burnett

There are a lot of great technicians in advertising. And unfortunately, they talk the best game. They know all the rules ... but there's one little rub. They forget that advertising is persuasion, and persuasion is not a science, but an art. Advertising is the art of persuasion. – William Bernbach

Facts and figures alone won't win over most consumers today. Personality and connection will. – Lee Rowley

*You can fix anything but a blank page.*

Nora Roberts

One of the biggest issues I see with client offers is an incongruence between the message and the intended market. That will ALWAYS cause conversion issues! – Jason Hornung

Everything in writing begins with language. Language begins with listening. – Jeanette Winterson

Dullness won't sell your product, but neither will irrelevant brilliance. – William Bernbach

I think a sentence is a fine thing to put a preposition at the end of. – William Zinsser

In our factory we make lipstick. In our advertising we sell hope. – Charles Revson

Copywriting is way more than putting words onto a screen. … [the] context and situation that influence the copy is called user experience. – Neil Patel

Writing begets writing. The more you write, the more writing you'll do and the easier it gets. – Ben Settle

I am in the poison gas business. Advertising should make you choke, make your eyes water, make you feel sick. – George Lois

Real content marketing isn't repurposed advertising, it is making something worth talking about. – Seth Godin

An essential aspect of creativity is not being afraid to fail. – Edwin Land

Content is anything that adds value to the reader's life. – Avinash Kaushik

This is the copywriter's task: not to create mass desire — but to channel and direct it. – Eugene Schwartz

Poor copy cannot overcome faults or gaps in dealer distribution; it cannot even cash in on the finest dealer setups. But good copy can, and does, surmount many dealer difficulties, making them secondary, and selling in spite of them. – Victor Schwab

A synonym is a word you use when you can't spell the other one. – Baltasar Gracián

*There is
no such thing
as too long.
Only too boring.*

Dan Kennedy

People rarely buy features. People sometimes buy benefits. People always buy emotion. – Anonymous

Content isn't what it is, content is what it does. – Jim Edwards

Consistency is key. Whenever you start, give your audience something to look forward to. – Julia McCoy

Bringing copywriters in at the end of the creative process is like trying to put toothpaste into a tube. – John Steinbeck

Copy must be believable. – Helen Landsdowne Resor

The idea is to write it so that people hear it and it slides through the brain and goes straight to the heart. – Maya Angelou

No, I don't think a 68-year-old copywriter . . . can write with the kids. That he's as creative. That he's as fresh. But he may be a better surgeon. His ad may not be quite as fresh and glowing as the Madison Ave. fraternity would like to see it be, and yet he might write an ad that will produce five times the sales. And that's the name of the game, isn't it? – Rosser Reeves

The often overlooked subhead is really a stealthy and lethal ninja writing weapon just sitting there quietly waiting to be put to good use. – Gary Korisko

In most agencies, account executives outnumber the copywriters two to one. If you were a dairy farmer would you employ twice as many milkers as you have cows? – David Ogilvy

When you start with what's at stake for the buyer, you earn the right to their attention. – Jake Sorofman

You can't wait for inspiration. You have to go after it with a club. – Jack London

Conversational copywriting doesn't feel dangerous to readers. – Nick Usborne

To impress your offer on the mind of the reader or listener, it is necessary to put it into brief, simple language…No farfetched or obscure statement will stop them. You have got to hit them where they live in the heart or in the head. You have got to catch their eyes or ears with something simple, something direct, something they want. – John Caples

The best marketing doesn't feel like marketing. – Tom Fishburne

*Don't push people to where you want them to be; meet them where they are.*

Meghan Keaney Anderson

Half my life is an act of revision. – John Irving

Why waste a sentence saying nothing? – Seth Godin

Don't fall in love with the products or services you're writing about, fall in love with the customers who need those products and services. – Scott Frothingham

If you're not embarrassed by your first version, you spent too long on it. – Reid Hoffman

One good idea, clearly and convincingly presented, is better than a dozen so–so ideas strung together. – Mark Ford

There is no such thing as a boring subject. Only boring, unimaginative writers. – Ben Hurt

Description begins in the writer's imagination, but should finish in the reader's. – Stephen King

Style means the right word. The rest matters little. – Jules Renard

Tell a story. Make it true. Make it compelling. And make it relevant. – Rand Fishkin

On your path to "X, Y, Z," it just makes sense to start with "A, B, C." – Stefanie Flaxman

I want my sales copy to feel like they're watching a movie (in their heads) about something that's super fascinating to them. So it's not just a lecture or dry facts — it's an experience. Something they can't get out of their heads until they buy …" – Ben Settle

Writing's a lot like cooking. Sometimes the cake won't rise, no matter what you do, and every now and again the cake tastes better than you ever could have dreamed it would. – Neil Gaiman

Your skillset is not half as important as your mindset. – Farnoosh Brock

It's just a matter of knowing what you're talking about, knowing the product and having a story, having a hook, having a great headline and lead, a strong close, bullets, testimonials … it's always the same. – Matt Furey

A gifted product is mightier than a gifted pen. – Gary Bencivenga

*You're never writing
for yourself
or the brand
that's paying you.
You're writing
for the reader.
A living, breathing
human being.*

*Paul
Hewerdine*

A copywriter should have an understanding of people, an insight into them, a sympathy towards them. – George Gribbin

Good writing is often about letting go of fear and affectation. – Stephen King

Instead of creating aesthetically pleasing prose, you have to dig into a product or service, uncover the reasons why consumers would want to buy the product, and present those sales arguments in copy that is read, understood, and reacted to—copy that makes the arguments so convincingly the customer can't help but want to buy the product being advertised. – Bob Bly

My first sentences are so short, they almost aren't sentences. – Joseph Sugarman

Even if you wind up throwing out 99% of it. That 1% could be a gold mine. – Phyllis Robinson

The most important thing is a hungry market not a brilliant burger. – Gary Halbert

Aim for complexity of thought, not expression. – Noah Lukeman

Imagine your letter being read by a guy in an apartment in Cleveland, in the midst of a ferocious winter storm, with gusting winds and snow outside at thigh height. You've got to get him so excited that he'll get out of the chair in front of the fireplace, bundle up, slog through the snow, go out to his cold car, and drive down to the post office to get a money order and a stamp to send his order in — rather than take the risk of waiting until tomorrow. – Dan Kennedy

Your message should single out your prospect like a man being paged in a crowded hotel lobby. – Claude Hopkins

Creativity is more than just being different. Anybody can play weird; that's easy. What's hard is to be as simple as Bach. Making the simple, awesomely simple, that's creativity. – Charles Mingus

Don't dismiss the power of caffeine and headphones. – Anonymous

The most important skill any marketer can master is copywriting. All marketing comes down to the marketer's ability to translate a "big idea" into a tight, easy-to-consume package. – Ryan Deiss

Humans are not ideally set up to understand logic; they are ideally set up to understand stories. – Roger C. Schank

People only buy when they're ready to buy. Not when you're ready to sell. – Drayton Bird

The most frequent reason for unsuccessful advertising is advertisers who are so full of their own accomplishments (the world's best seed!) that they forget to tell us why we should buy (the world's best lawn!). – John Caples

The easy, conversational tone of good writing comes only on the eighth rewrite. – Paul Graham

Don't waste time looking for a better pencil: learn to write better. – Seth Godin

Pockets are the most sensitive part of a human being; that's why we need to touch hearts and minds first. –Lula da Silva

The perfect advertisement is one of which the reader can say: "This is for me, and for me alone." – Peter Drucker

The first draft is just you telling yourself the story. – Terry Pratchett

*The only writer
to whom you should
compare yourself
is the writer
you were
yesterday.*

David Schlosser

The most essential gift for a good writer is a built–in, shock–protected bullshit detector. – Ernest Hemingway

Your job as a writer means placing enough information in front of your audience that they can see your point, rather than be utterly swayed to it. It's critical to know your audience well so that you don't over- or under-persuade. – James Chartrand

Creativity. The more you use, the more you have. – Anonymous

Something you know about your customer may be more important than anything you know about your product. – Harvey McKay

Fun without sell gets nowhere, but sell without fun tends to become obnoxious. – Leo Burnett

No one can write decently who is distrustful of the reader's intelligence or whose attitude is patronizing. – E. B. White

When people go to a web page, the thing that they want more than anything else is instant clarity. – Ken McCarthy

Writer's block doesn't exist…lack of imagination does. – Cyrese Covelli

In writing, rhythm is defined by punctuation and the stress patterns of words in a sentence. Long sentences sound smoother, while short sentences make your content snappier. – Henneke Duistermaat

The first thing is to have the attention of the reader. That means to be interesting. The next thing is to stick to the truth, and that means rectifying whatever's wrong in the merchant's business. If the truth isn't tellable, fix it so it is. That is about all there is to it. – John E. Powers

Write drunk; edit sober. – Ernest Hemingway

Advertisers will do practically anything to get you to click on their ads, but all they really need to do is make your life easier, cut the crap, and get to the point. – Dan Shewan

When your story is ready for rewrite, cut it to the bone. Get rid of every ounce of excess fat. This is going to hurt; revising a story down to the bare essentials is always a little like murdering children, but it must be done. – Stephen King

People will see right through your fluff and filler. – Neil Patel

Vanilla doesn't attract clients. Your special flavor is what your 5-Star Clients want. – Jeanna Gabellini

A professional writer is an amateur who didn't quit. – Richard Bach

Good content always has an objective; it's created with intent. It, therefore, carries triggers to action. – Ann Handley

Sell a good night's sleep, not the mattress. – Anonymous

The first draft of everything is shit. – Ernest Hemingway

Anyone who says writing is easy isn't doing it right. – Amy Joy

Editing might be a bloody trade, but knives aren't the exclusive property of butchers. Surgeons use them too. – Blake Morrison

Everyone is interested in what's new. Few people are interested in what's better. – Al Ries

*Repeat the mantra:
Writing is when
I make the words.
Editing is when
I make them
not shitty.*

Chuck Wendig

It is perfectly okay to write garbage — as long as you edit brilliantly. – C. J. Cherryh

Content should ask people to do something and reward them for it. – Lee Odden

Personally, I am very fond of strawberries and cream, but I have found that for some strange reason, fish prefer worms. – Dale Carnegie

You can't just place a few "Buy" buttons on your website and expect your visitors to buy. – Neil Patel

Give yourself three drafts to produce great work. Make the first one crappy, the next one good, and the final one excellent. This'll keep your writing efficient and clear, and you won't get lost in a series of random drafts. – Neville Medhora

I have only made this letter longer because I have not had the time to make it shorter. – Blaise Pascal

Write with conviction. Pick a side and be bold. And if you're wrong, admit it. – Jeff Goins

Write without fear. Edit without mercy. – Natasha Al-Atassi

You cannot educate people into buying your product. – Josh Earl

For a long time now I have tried simply to write the best I can. Sometimes I have good luck and write better than I can. – Ernest Hemingway

On average, 8 out of 10 people will read your headline copy, but only 2 out 10 will read the rest. – Brian Clark

Quality content means content that is packed with clear utility and is brimming with inspiration, and it has relentless empathy for the audience. – Ann Handley

Every sale has five basic obstacles: no need, no money, no hurry, no desire, no trust. – Zig Ziglar

Writing is the only thing that, when I do it, I don't feel I should be doing something else. – Gloria Steinem

Clarity trumps conciseness when I'm editing copy since the goal is to persuade the reader to take a next step. – Rennie Sansui

There are three objectives for content marketing: reach, engagement, conversion. Define key metrics for each. – Michael Brenner

Nothing sticks in your head better than a story. Stories can express the most complicated ideas in the most digestible ways. – Sam Balter, Sr.

Even though you are on the right track, you'll get run over if you just sit there. – Will Rogers

At its very core, marketing is storytelling. The best advertising campaigns take us on an emotional journey — appealing to our wants, needs, and desires — while at the same time telling us about a product or service. – Melinda Partin

Get a fix on the prospect/customer/client and on his or her desires; failing to do so will undermine all your other efforts. – Dan Kennedy

Start writing, no matter what. The water does not flow until the faucet is turned on. – Louis L'Amour

*If your stories are all about your products and services, that's not storytelling.
It's a brochure.
Give yourself permission to make the story bigger.*

Jay Baer

Let's get to the heart of the matter. The power, the force, the overwhelming urge to own that makes advertising work, comes from the market itself, and not from the copy. Copy cannot create desire for a product. It can only take the hopes, dreams, fears and desires that already exist in the hearts of millions of people, and focus those already existing desires onto a particular product. This is the copy writer's task: not to create this mass desire – but to channel and direct it. – Eugene Schwartz

Professional writers don't have muses; they have mortgages. – Larry Kahaner

Tomorrow may be hell, but today was a good writing day, and on the good writing days nothing else matters. – Neil Gaiman

Do you know what is the most-often missing ingredient in a sales message? It's the sales message that doesn't tell an interesting story. Storytelling…good storytelling…is a vital component of a marketing campaign. – Gary Halbert

Virality is like catching lightning in a bottle. Instead, focus on what you can control like the conversion and the branding. – Daniel Harmon

Less is more. Keeping it simple takes time and effort. – Jeff Bullas

All writing is difficult. The most you can hope for is a day when it goes reasonably easily. Plumbers don't get plumber's block, and doctors don't get doctor's block; why should writers be the only profession that gives a special name to the difficulty of working, and then expects sympathy for it? – Philip Pullman

Knowing a lot of words is good, but using obscure words is bad. As Stephen King said, "Any word you have to hunt for in a thesaurus is the wrong word." This is as true for fiction as it is for business copy. – Brad Shorr

Content, in all its forms, is the single most critical element of any marketing campaign. – Rebecca Lieb

A barber lathers a man before he shaves him. – Dale Carnegie

In my experience, the number one key to persuasion is this: communicate trust. If you do this well, you at least have a chance at engaging and persuading the reader. If you don't do this well, however, no amount of fancy copywriting techniques will save you. – Steve Slaunwhite

Good stories surprise us. They make us think and feel. They stick in our minds and help us remember ideas and concepts in a way that a PowerPoint crammed with bar graphs never can. – Joe Lazauskas

If content is King, context is God. – Gary Vaynerchuk

People don't buy what you do, they buy why you do it. – Simon Sinek

Instead of one-way interruption, web marketing is about delivering useful content at just the precise moment that a buyer needs it. – David Meerman Scott

Use a pile driver. Hit the point once. Then come back and hit it again. Then hit it a third time — a tremendous whack. – Richard Perry

Advertising is based on one thing, happiness. And you know what happiness is? Happiness is the smell of a new car. It's freedom from fear. It's a billboard on the side of the road that screams reassurance that whatever you are doing is okay. You are okay. – Don Draper

Words are a puzzle; put them together the right way and you get something beautiful. – Amy Joy

Marketing is no longer about the stuff that you make, but about the stories you tell. – Seth Godin

*Don't tell stories about your product — change the stories the custmers tell about themselves.*

Ryan Deiss

Assume the reader knows nothing. But don't assume the reader is stupid. – Ann Handley

I'm always listening to my audience. It's not just content I throw out into the Internet, it's content answered to a specific need or question. – Sonja Jefferson

I am so happy that I made someone cry today - don't worry I'm a writer. It's when they make me cry that it's a problem. – Tina Smith

Beware, then, of the long word that is no better than the short word: "numerous" (many), "facilitate" (ease), "individual" (man or woman), "remainder" (rest), "initial" (first), "implement" (do), "sufficient" (enough), "attempt" (try), "referred to as" (called), and hundreds more. – William Zinsser

Here's who I am, here's what I have, here's why you want it… and here's what to do now. – John Carlton

My life is a constant battle between wanting to correct grammar and wanting to have friends. – Anonymous

A good ad doesn't just repeat facts. It dramatizes them. – Justin Oberman

Probably the biggest thing or biggest "aha" moment I had with the process of copywriting was when I realized that copywriting was more than just being creative. I used to think, "Wow, let's come up with something great and wonderful," and I didn't start becoming successful, in my own eyes, until I said, "No, my clients are not hiring me to be creative; they're hiring me to deliver a control." – Carline Anglade-Cole

We have to continually be jumping off cliffs and developing our wings on the way down. – Kurt Vonnegut, Jr.

When we create something, we think, "Will our customers thank us for this?" I think it's important for all of us to be thinking about whatever marketing we're creating; is it really useful to our customers? Will they thank us for it? I think if you think of things through that lens, it just clarifies what you're doing in such a simple, elegant way. – Ann Handley

Being a writer is 1% inspiration, 50% perspiration and 49% explaining you're not a millionaire like J. K.Rowling. – Gabrielle Tozer

Writing is thinking. To write well is to think clearly. That's why it's so hard. – David McCullough

If writing didn't require thinking then we'd all be doing it. – Jeremiah Laabs

Great marketers have immense empathy for their audience. They can put themselves in their shoes, live their lives, feel what they feel, go where they go, and respond how they'd respond. That empathy comes out in content that resonates with your audience. – Rand Fishkin

Creativity may well be the last legal unfair competitive advantage we can take to run over the competition. – William Bernbach

If your grammatically correct, carefully proofread sales spiel full of intricately detailed descriptions and long words nobody's ever heard of doesn't spark a discussion, then your content is shit. – Georgina Chapman

A copywriter isn't a writer who sells. A copywriter is a salesperson who writes. – Anonymous

Don't let your copy write checks that the product/service can't cash. - Scott Frothingham

Creativity and innovation are about finding unexpected solutions to obvious problems, or finding obvious solutions to unexpected problems. – Rei Inamoto

Words, once they are printed, have a life of their own – Carol Burnett

*Creative
that doesn't solve
a business problem
is a problem.*

Cabell
Harris

People believe what they want to believe. – Drayton Bird

Copy is not written. If anyone tells you "you write copy," sneer at them. Copy is not written. Copy is assembled. You do not write copy, you assemble it. You are working with a series of building blocks, you are putting the building blocks together, and then you are putting them in certain structures, you are building a little city of desire for your person to come and live in. – Eugene Schwartz

One idea to a sentence is still the best advice that anyone has ever given on writing. – Bill Bryson

I've advised many clients who feel compelled to use 'proper English' in their sales letters… to "fire your English teacher!" – David Garfinkel

Good marketing makes the company look smart. Great marketing makes the customer feel smart. – Joe Chernov

People rarely buy features. People sometimes by benefits. People always buy emotion. – Glenn Fisher

Every first draft is perfect because all the first draft has to do is exist. It's perfect in its existence. The only way it could be imperfect would be to NOT exist. – Jane Smiley

Long copy is OK. Long-winded copy is not OK – Neville Medhora

PASSION… Let your excitement and enthusiasm spill out all over the page. Don't hold back. Put that pen to the page and RAVE! – Gary Halbert

The difference between the almost right word and the right word is the difference between the lightning bug and the lightning. – Mark Twain

What really decides consumers to buy or not to buy is the content of your advertising, not its form. – David Ogilvy

Remember, people don't buy from you because they understand what you sell—they buy from you because they feel understood. – Dan Lok

A real writer learns from earlier writers the way a boy learns from an apple orchard — by stealing what he has a taste for, and can carry off. – Archibald MacLeish

A big reason so many businesses compete on price is because they can't prove what value they offer, so they're stuck with the one selling point that's a breeze to communicate: cheapness. – Mish Slade

> *The sole purpose of the first sentence in an advertisement is to get you to read the second sentence of the copy.*

Joseph Sugarman

Good advertising does not just circulate information. It penetrates the public mind with desires and belief. – Leo Burnett

If you wait for inspiration to write you're not a writer, you're a waiter. – Dan Poynter

How to write a good email: 1. Write your email. 2. Delete most of it. 3. Send. – Dan Munz

We are not selling technology. We are not selling the product. We are not selling you. We are selling peace of mind. – Dimitri Lambermont

If you are a copywriter's boss, please understand that a copywriter is working when they're staring out the window. – Scott Frothingham

An idea can turn to dust or magic, depending on the talent that rubs against it. – William Bernbach

Do something. If it works, do more of it. If it doesn't, do something else. – Franklin D. Roosevelt

No one wants to be lectured or told what to do. – Tucker Max

Content marketing is the gap between what brands produce and what consumers actually want. –Michael Brenner

Translating BIG IDEAS into as few words as possible is the essence of great copywriting. – Ryan Deiss

Clichés can be quite fun. That's how they got to be clichés. – Alan Bennett

I am one who believes that one of the greatest dangers of advertising is not that of misleading people, but that of boring them to death. – Leo Burnett

Creative people are 50% ego and 50% insecurity. – Lee Clow

The very first thing you must come to realize is that you must become a "student of markets." Not products. Not techniques. Not copywriting. Not how to buy space or whatever. Now, of course, all of these things are important and you must learn about them, but, the first and the most important thing you must learn is what people want to buy. – Gary Halbert

Throw up into your typewriter every morning. Clean up every noon. – Raymond Chandler

Content that wins is the content that the consumers will talk about. That's the test. – Jay Baer

Being a writer requires an intoxication with language. – Jim Harrison

Our job is to bring the dead facts to life. – William Bernbach

Three things need to happen; attention, connection, action. – Kevin Rogers

The attention economy is not growing, which means we have to grab the attention that someone else has today. – Brent Leary

Don't filter yourself. Just get it down on paper and don't hold back. Not even genius copywriters write compelling copy off the top of their heads; they reject 99% of their other ideas first. - Jacqueline Phillips

Use words – all words – with an eye, ear, and nose for the odor of skunk. If you're not sure how a reader will interpret or respond to a word … if it's possibly confusing, ambiguous, or offensive … that's your signal to look for a different way of saying it. – Will Newman

*When it comes to writing, clarity trumps all rules.*

C. E. McLean

One should not aim at being possible to understand, but at being impossible to misunderstand. – F. L. Lucas

If what you're writing isn't fun, then throw it out and write something that is fun. It should never feel like a chore if you do it right. – Ben Settle

Make 'em curious. People simply cannot stand having a secret kept from them. This psychological law is one of the most powerful driving forces behind many of the most successful copywriting controls ever. – Jo Han Mok

The ideas presented in your copy should flow in a logical fashion, anticipating your prospect's questions and answering them as if the questions were asked face–to–face. – Joseph Sugarman

Why aren't the thinks I'm thinking getting thunk on the page any faster?!? – Christopher Lehman

Your top of the funnel content must be intellectually divorced from your product but emotionally wed to it. – Joe Chernov

Attention is the currency. – Gary Vaynerchuk

Even today you can look through almost any consumer or professional publication and find headlines that possess not a single one of the necessary qualities, such as self-interest, news, or curiosity. – John Caples

Most of my work consisted of crossing out. Crossing out was the secret of all good writing. – Mark Haddon

A good story often increases the salability of an item without increasing its actual value. – Roy H. Williams

I don't know how to speak to everybody, only to somebody. – Howard Gossage

I can write better than anybody who can write faster, and I can write faster than anybody who can write better. – A. J. Liebling

Brilliant copywriting won't sell a turd. – Doberman Dan

You can't think yourself out of a writing block; you have to write yourself out of a thinking block. – John Rogers

Remember that the reader's attention is yours for only a single, involuntary instant. They will not use up their valuable time trying to figure out what you mean. They will simply turn the page. – John Caples

Get it down. Take chances. It may be bad, but it's the only way you can do anything good. – William Faulkner

Decide the effect you want to produce in your reader. – Robert Collier

It's not enough to convince prospects you have a great product or a superior service. You must also show them that the value of your offer far exceeds the price you are asking for it. – Bob Bly

Swap places with your readers. – Ann Handley

I think clarity starts with having (a few questions) really clear in your mind: "What is this blog post about and what am I going to teach my readers with it? How will it make them feel once they've learned this?" –Henneke Duistermaat

I would advise anyone who aspires to a writing career that before developing his talent he would be wise to develop a thick hide. – Harper Lee

*I don't know the rules of grammar. If you're trying to persuade people to do something, or buy something, it seems to me you should use their language.*

David Ogilvy

Any fool can make something complicated. It takes a genius to make it simple. — Woody Guthrie

Instead of all the wealth buried in any gold mine I'll settle for just one profitable sales letter. It's far more valuable! — Gary Halbert

If you can take your personality and inject it into the message you share, you'll be one step ahead in the content marketing game. — Jason Miller

The difference between a writer and someone who writes is that the former enlightens the reader while the latter confuses the reader. — Brad Shorr

The world's most powerful business tool is also the most misunderstood. The e-factors are all about feelings not figures and feelings rule all buying decisions! — Daniel C. Felsted

If you are writing about baloney, don't try and make it Cornish hen, because that's the worst kind of baloney there is. Just make it darn good baloney. — Leo Burnett

You want to solve the pain point for the customer. — Anthony Melleka

Presenting something unexpected – breaking a pattern – will help you to capture attention, according to research. This works in two parts: surprise captures our attention initially, and interest holds it. Why is this so powerful? Surprises are more stimulating for us. – Bella Beth Cooper

Serious writers are warriors of the pen who leverage fear to their advantage. When perfection and fearlessness are set aside, what's left is purpose and focus. – Bryan Hutchinson

If I said that Pablo Escobar was rich, you wouldn't take much note. If I said he spent $2,500 monthly, on rubber bands needed to hold stacks of bills together, you'd say "Wow, that guy was rich!" That is what good copy does. – Hannah Lipschutz

Understand the power of asking. – Drayton Bird

Good writing is supposed to evoke sensation in the reader – not the fact that it is raining, but the feeling of being rained upon. – E. L. Doctorow

Your content core connects the dots between what your customers care about and what your business has to offer them. – Garrett Moon

All ideas grow out of other ideas. – Anish Kapoor

Starting the writing process is about staring at the blank paper/screen and not getting frustrated by the fact that you have no fucking idea what to put there. – Brett Snyder

When you don't give your customers enough information, the right information, or put it where it needs to be on the page, you run the risk of giving them the impression that you care more about the sale than them. – Jenifer Havice

Avoid weasel words — words like maybe, hope and perhaps that are a bit weak and don't 'command' action. – Gail Goodman

Emotions are the fire of human motivation, the combustible force that secretly drives most decisions to buy. When your marketing harnesses those forces correctly you will generate explosive increases in response. – Gary Bencivenga

The more your copy sounds like a real conversation, the more engaging it will be. – David Garfinkel

A good ad should be like a good sermon: It must not only comfort the afflicted, it also must afflict the comfortable. – Bernice Fitz-Gibbon

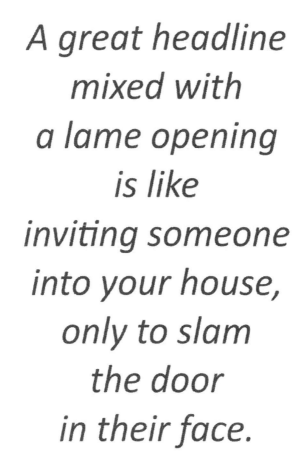

*A great headline
mixed with
a lame opening
is like
inviting someone
into your house,
only to slam
the door
in their face.*

Brian Clark

If you can quit, then quit. If you can't quit, you're a writer. – R. A. Salvatore

We laugh at automated writing because we know that copywriting is really copy*thinking*. We're not mere word-arrangers; that's just the part of the iceberg you can see. – Tom Albrighton

The only way to win at content marketing is for the reader to say, "This was written specifically for me." – Jamie Turner

We are not in the business of being original. We are in the business of reusing things that work. – Bob Bly

Don't focus on having a great blog. Focus on having a blog that's great for your readers. – Brian Clark

Hard writing makes easy reading. Easy writing makes hard reading. – William Zinsser

Once somebody is on your landing page, you want to start a conversation with them. – Dave Gerhardt

We sell to creatures of emotion, bristling with prejudice, and motivated by pride and vanity. – Dale Carnegie

Advertising is the "wonder" in Wonder Bread. – Jef I. Richards

Top–flight sales copy is never a cost. It's a profit center. – Clayton Makepeace

In any art you're allowed to steal anything if you can make it better. – Ernest Hemingway

Being a copywriter is basically rewriting the same sentence seven times just to avoid writing the word "solution." – Katherine Wildman

Value is best communicated when it's designed to be believed, not just described. – Bernadette Jiwa

Do you know what is the most–often missing ingredient in a sales message? It's the sales message that doesn't tell an interesting story. Storytelling…good storytelling…is a vital component of a marketing campaign. – Gary Halbert

A small admission gains a large acceptance. – William  Bernbach

I never met a word I didn't love. – Gail Carson Levine

If you want to understand how a lion hunts, don't go to the zoo. Go to the jungle. – Jim Stengel

Too often, marketers view copy as a sales pitch and not as an opportunity for revealing their brand -- whether that's by infusing a little humor, speaking more casually or demonstrating thought leadership. – Amanda Hinski

Storytelling offers the opportunity to talk with your audience, not at them. People can't help but want to be a part of your story, and that's how marketing can happen the natural way. – Laura Holloway

The beautiful part of writing is that you don't have to get it right the first time, unlike, say, a brain surgeon. – Robert Cormier

Make the customer the hero of your story. – Ann Handley

The best brands are built on great stories. – Ian Rowden

> *When you don't give your customers enough information, the right information or put it where it needs to be on the page, you run the risk of giving them the impression that you care more about the sale than them.*

Jennifer
Havice

Use low commitment CTAs [in emails]. Emails are invites, landing pages are parties. – Matt Byrd

Every word, sentence, and headline should have one specific purpose – to lead your potential customer to your order page. – Shelley Lowery

If a period is a stop sign, then what kind of traffic flow is created by other marks? The comma is a speed bump; the semicolon is what a driver education teacher calls a "rolling stop"; the parenthetical expression is a detour; the colon is a flashing yellow light that announces something important up ahead; the dash is a tree branch in the road. – Roy Peter Clark

Everyone – no exceptions – responds to well–written, persuasive, emotionally based copy. Not everyone can write it, that's why copywriters are often paid so much, but no one can escape its power. – Joe Vitale

A confused mind never buys. – John Childers

The aim of marketing is to know and understand the customer so well that the product or service fits him or her and sells itself. – Peter Drucker

Craft your headline based on the frustration of your target market. What keeps them awake at night? If you know exactly what makes them tick, you can create a headline that goes straight for the jugular. – Jo Han Mok

So the writer who breeds more words than he needs, is making a chore for the reader who reads. – Dr. Seuss

Some writers are uncomfortable with the concept of a hard sales pitch; other writers are uncomfortable with "boring" assignments. Great writers are uncomfortable with not writing. – Brad Shorr

Sometimes the most important job advertising can do, is to clarify the obvious. – Jay Chiat

All you have to do is put one word after another, and remember how great it feels to be a writer. – Stephanie Lennox

Always tell your prospects what to do next. – Scott Frothingham

Great emails go unopened, great videos go unwatched, and great articles never get read because their headline sucks. – Dennis Yu

The key to good writing is to leave Boo Radley in the house until the end of the story. – Michael P. Naughton

You don't have to get it perfect, you just have to get it going. – Gary Halbert

I've found the best way to revise your own work is to pretend that somebody else wrote it and then to rip the living shit out of it. – Don Roff

You can say the right thing about a product and nobody will listen. You've got to say it in such a way that people will feel it in their gut. Because if they don't feel it, nothing will happen. – William Bernbach

Think of your words as money; your goal is to spend wisely so that you maximize the return on your investment. – Brett Snyder

I hereby grant you permission to write crap. The more the better. Remember, crap makes the best fertilizer. – Pat Pattison

Cut out all these exclamation points. An exclamation point is like laughing at your own joke. – F. Scott Fitzgerald

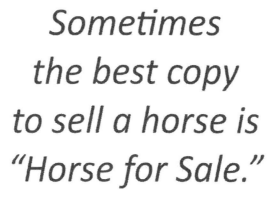

*Sometimes
the best copy
to sell a horse is
"Horse for Sale."*

Jay Abraham

I don't want my writing to sound like the way we were taught to write. Because I don't want you to be aware of my writing. – Elmore Leonard

Content Marketing is a commitment, not a campaign. – Jon Buscall

The main things you want to tap into are relevancy, relatability, and emotion. – Daniel Harmon

Almost all the advice you get is wrong – because people overcomplicate matters. – Drayton Bird

I just rearrange words into a pleasing order for money. – Terry Pratchett

Make your copy straightforward to read, understand and use. Use easy words; those that are used for everyday speech. Use phrases that are not too imprecise and very understandable. Do not be too stuffy; remove pompous words and substitute them with plain words. Minimize complicated gimmicks and constructions. If you can't give the data directly and briefly, you must consider writing the copy again. – Jay Abraham

Words are how we think, story is how we link. – Christina Baldwin

The great fun in my life has been getting up every morning and rushing to the typewriter because some new idea has hit me. – Ray Bradbury

The first step in persuasion is to entice your target to imagine doing the thing you want them to do. – Roy H. Williams

There are two typos of people in this world: those who can edit and those who can't. – Jarod Kintz

When your customers feel that you're talking to them on a deep emotional level and understand their hopes, fears, and desires better than the competition, you're gonna get the sale. – Adam Kreitmann

The only kind of writing is rewriting. – Ernest Hemingway

There are tons of different factors that go into ranking well (in search), but the biggest is high–quality content. – David Sinick

You have to write about something you care about and do it in a way that your people care about. Be entertaining and useful or just really damn useful! – Sonia Simone

Hear this: If you wanna win (make moolah) at email marketing, read the following five words very carefully and take them to heart. Stop Branding and Start Selling. – Kelvin Dorsey

To swear off making mistakes is very easy. All you have to do is to swear off having ideas. – Leo Burnett

Once you've gotten your prospect's attention, they want to know that you understand their problems and that you have solved that same type of problems in the past. Then they want to know what you have to offer that will create those same type of results for them. – Scott Frothingham

The secret to good writing is to use small words for big ideas, not to use big words for small ideas. – Oliver Markus

Write. Rewrite. When not writing or rewriting, read. I know of no shortcuts. – Larry L. King

Good writing serves the reader, not the writer. It isn't self-indulgent. Good writing anticipates the questions that readers might have as they're reading a piece, and it answers them. – Ann Handley

Content: there is no easy button. – Scott Abel

> *You know you're writing well when you're throwing good stuff into the wastebasket.*

Ernest Hemingway

Adventure, comedy/humor, emotion, inspiration, and surprise (cats, dogs, and babies). All of these things have 1 thing in common: they make you feel something, not think something. – Jay Shetty

You can always edit a bad page. You can't edit a blank page. – Jodi Picoult

Your prospects need a reason behind your product based on three factors: why your product is the best, why your prospects should believe you and why they need to buy the product right now. – Brian Clark

No matter what your content is about, if someone clicks through to see your content, they're looking for an answer to something. Rather than giving them the runaround, give them what they're looking for. Answer their question simply and clearly and with as little jargon as possible. – Kevin Ho

There's no such thing as writer's block. That was invented by people in California who couldn't write. – Terry Pratchett

Traditional marketing talks at people. Content marketing talks with them. – Doug Kessler

The truth connects the dots between people and purchase. – Scott Frothingham

Humble yourself and truly serve your audience, listen to their needs and desires, listen to the language they use. If you listen carefully, your audience can eventually give you everything you need, including much of your copy. Get out of their way. – Robert Bruce

Because business decisions are also based on feelings, writers must be able to provoke an emotional response in many of their assignments. Warm prospects freeze when exposed to cold writing. – Brad Shorr

Be vivid. Tell a story. Don't be bland. – Seth Godin

Content marketing is really like a first date. If all you do is talk about yourself, there won't be a second date. – David Beebe

Do not worship at the altar of creativity. – David Ogilvy

If you can just support the emotions that they're feeling, and you can do it with integrity—you really do have the solution—then you don't really ever have to sell hard, or even push to sell. – Ray Edwards

Art is never finished, only abandoned. – Leonardo da Vinci

When you're not able to articulate the direction you want your content to take your readers, it's difficult for your readers to understand where you're taking them, too. – Meera Kothand

Short copy actually takes longer to write. That's why I go through so many drafts; because it's a process of distillation. You start with 25 gallons of sour mash to produce a fifth of whiskey. – Jim Punkre

Words are loaded pistols. – Jean Paul Sartre

Only one kind of person in the world gets to decide whether you rule or suck: Prospects who cast their votes by responding to your copy in the only way that matters – by spending their own hard-earned money. – Clayton Makepeace

They do enjoy a good story, they do enjoy being sold by a good salesman. They just don't like the feel like they're being unfairly manipulated. – David L. Deutsch

If you have an important point to make, don't try to be subtle or clever . . . Hit the point once. Then come back and hit it again. Then hit it a third time—a tremendous whack! – Winston Churchill

*There is no perfect time to write. There's only now.*

Barbara Kingsolver

Avoid jargon. Nothing says you're a bullshitter more than using language that's designed to obscure, not clarify. Speak in plain-English. – George Tannenbaum

Be courageous and try to write in a way that scares you a little. – Holly Gerth

Our job is to use real people's words to express what they want, what they like, what they need. It's to make it clear that we don't have what they don't want. – Joanna Wiebe

Tell the readers a story! Because without a story, you are merely using words to prove you can string them together in logical sentences. – Anne McCaffrey

Strong copy should help leverage the thoughts and feelings that are already rolling around in your prospect's head ... and help him realize it's time to take action in his best interest. – Donnie Bryant

The Six Golden Rules of Writing: Read, read, read, and write, write, write. – Ernest Gaines

Perfectionism is the voice of the oppressor, the enemy of the people. It will keep you cramped and insane your whole life. – Anne Lamott

I just give myself permission to suck. I delete about 90 percent of my first drafts… so it doesn't really matter much if on a particular day I write beautiful and brilliant prose that will stick in the minds of my readers forever, because there's a 90 percent chance I'm just gonna delete whatever I write anyway. I find this hugely liberating. – John Green

People don't like to be addressed as a crowd. They prefer to read something that addresses them personally, directly. — Henneke Duistermaat

Real copywriting is the deconstruction of marketing goals, and the construction of salesmanship. – John Carlton

The only way I can get anything written at all is to write really, really shitty first drafts. The first draft is the child's draft, where you let it all pour out and then let it romp all over the place, knowing that no one is going to see it and that you can shape it later. – Anne Lamott

When a thought takes one's breath away, a grammar lesson seems an impertinence. – Thomas W. Higginson

At the end of the day your ability to connect with your readers comes down to how you make them feel. – Benjamin J. Carey

But at its core marketing is about getting someone's attention by invoking emotion, inspiring action and belief, and persuading someone to take the leap. – Mark Kilens

I'm not a very good writer, but I'm an excellent re-writer. – James Michener

Referring to an event in an untold story is a powerful technique rarely used. – Roy H. Williams

If you want to be a writer, you must do two things above all others: read a lot and write a lot. – Stephen King

I love deadlines. I like the whooshing sound they make as they fly by. – Douglas Adams

Actually talk to your customers. Use the language that they use. Talk about the things they talk about. Never feed salad to a lion. – Jay Acunzo

Often the success of your copy hinges your ability to transfer enthusiasm. – Scott Frothingham

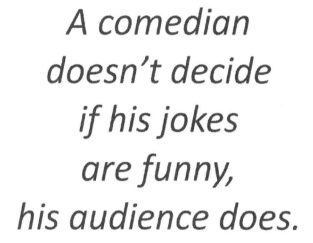

*A comedian doesn't decide if his jokes are funny, his audience does.*

Patrick Bet-David

Storytelling uses a few basic elements: a beginning, a conflict, a climax, an end. If one of those is missing, it isn't a story – it's just the description of an event. – James Chartrand

We know how to sniff out a sales pitch when it's coming our way, and we often resent it. – Lianna Patch

Copywriting, as you may have already discovered, is not easy. Even for the pros. Yup, some days writing copy you will feel as frustrated as a cat trying to bury a turd on a marble floor. – Kelvin Dorsey

My favorite-est question to ask before creating content is "what should the audience *be able to do* afterward?" – Tamsen Webster

But nobody will do what they need to do. People only do what they want to do. Sell people what they want, not what they need. And if you want to make big money and make a significant impact on someone's life...include what they need WITH what they want. – Jim Edwards

Some people HATE this news: you'll never get better at writing copy without falling in love with research. – Joel Klettke

Passive voice makes you sound weak, reactive, or acted upon, while active voice takes charge. – Helen Nesterenko

Advertising doesn't create a product advantage. It can only convey it…No matter how skillful you are, you can't invent a product advantage that doesn't exist. – William Bernbach

It's not just our ability to deliver a positive outcome for a customer that determines success, it's also our ability to intensify the positive expectation of delight to follow. – Robert Rose

Understanding WHY your fellow humans like and share and care (or don't care) about the things being put in front of them is essential to succeeding as a copywriter. – Kevin Rogers

Write choppy copy. Short sentences work great. Each line should play off of each other. You don't need to finish every thought in every line. – Dave Gerhardt

We've had it educated out of us in grammar school, university, and god help you if you've been to a business school. You end up writing in a way no one can understand. – Nick Usborne

Think of every sentence like a rung on a ladder. Word each of those steps in such a way as to make them want to take the NEXT step... and the NEXT... all the way to your order button... or whatever's the next step in your sales process. – Drew Eric Whitman

*Here's everything you need to know about creating killer content in 3 simple words: Clear. Concise. Compelling.*

Demian Farnworth

Ideas are cheap. It's the execution that is all important. – George R.R. Martin

Valuable content is found at the intersection between your customer's needs and your business expertise. – Sonja Jefferson

Just know that this frustration is normal, that all creative professionals feel tired and discouraged from time to time, especially in the beginning. The only way to find success is to continuously study your craft and never quit. – Eddie Shleyner

A problem with a piece of writing often clarifies itself if you go for a long walk. – Helen Dunmore

What is it that most ad copywriters lack? The ability to marry relevance and credibility to inspire the reader to make a purchase. – Alex Mandossian

The nearest I have to a rule is a Post-it on the wall in front of my desk saying 'Faire et se taire' from Flaubert. Which I translate for myself as 'Shut up and get on with it.' – Helen Simpson

Don't tell me how good you make it; tell me how good it makes me when I use it. – Leo Burnett

# R. Scott Frothingham
Wordwrangler. Carrotdangler. Storyteller.

 Ever since 5th grade, when he won a prize for reciting a poem in a school assembly, Scott has been hooked on writing that gets a reaction. That's what has driven him through careers in broadcasting and publishing and brought him to full-time copy and content writing where his focus is helping businesses tell their story and writing copy that converts.

Comments? Questions?
Suggested Quotes to Add to the Next Edition of this book?
Contact Scott at LinkedIn: www.linkedin.com/in/scottfrothingham
or ScottFroth@FastForwardResults.com

# Robert W. Bly

 For 4 decades, Bob has been writing high-performance direct response copy for IBM, AT&T, Intuit, Forbes, Medical Economics, ITT, and dozens of other smart direct marketers, both large and small, who want to get more leads and sales -- online and offline.

McGraw-Hill calls Bob Bly "America's top copywriter." The Direct Marketing Association awarded him the Gold Echo, and AWAI voted Bob Copywriter of the Year. He writes a column for Target Marketing magazine, has taught copywriting at New York University, and is the author of 100 published books, including *The Digital Marketing Handbook* (Entrepreneur Press) and *The Copywriter's Handbook* (Henry Holt).

# My Top 12

 When flipping through this book looking for inspiration or motivation, you might stumble across quotes that resonate with you on a deeper level than the others. Write those quotes down here so you can always have, fast easy access.

1. _____

_____

_____

2. _____

_____

_____

3. _____

_____

_____

4. _____

_____

_____

5. _____

_____

_____

6. _____

_____

_____

7. _____

_____

_____

8. _____

_____

_____

9. _____

_____

_____

10.

_____

_____

_____

11. _____

_____

_____

12. _____

_____

_____

## Playing Favorites

You're being interviewed. You are asked, "What is your favorite quote about writing?" You respond:

_____

_____

_____

"What's your favorite book/author about copywriting?"

_____

_____

_____

"What's your favorite book/author NOT about copywriting?"

_____

_____

_____

The answers to these three questions say a lot about how you approach your craft. Write them down here and periodically revisit them. Don't be surprised if your favorites change over time.

# Hey! What about these?

If you're familiar with some great quotes for copywriters that didn't make this edition, send 'em in with a suggestion that they be included in the next edition.

1. _____

_____

_____

2. _____

_____

_____

3. _____

_____

_____

4. _____

_____

_____

5. _____

_____

_____

6. _____

_____

_____

Send your suggestions to Scott at LinkedIn: https://www.linkedin.com/in/scottfrothingham/

# Got something to say?

 Have you authored quotable quotes that could help inspire or motivate a fellow copywriter? Spread the love. Send 'em to Scott with a request to include 'em in the next edition to https://www.linkedin.com/in/scottfrothingham

1. _____

_____

_____

_____

2. _____

_____

_____

_____

3. _____

_____

_____

_____

4. _____

_____

_____

# Who Are These People?

 Sometimes a great quote can be more interesting if you know something about the person who said it or the context in which it was said. Jot down the names of people you want to learn more about because of what they said or how they said it.

For example, you like the quote by Clayton Makepeace on page 96. Make a note of his name so, when you have the time you can search and find out, among other things, that over the past 40 years, his marketing strategies, sales copy and art direction have created more than three million new customers for his clients and generated more than $1.5 billion in sales. This might lead you to check to see if Makepeace has any books or courses that could help you improve your craft.

1. _____

2. _____

3. _____

4. _____

5. _____

6. _____

7. _____

8. _____

9. _____

10. _____

# Where to Find a Quote from a Favorite Writer
alphabetical by last name with page number(s)

# BONUS CONTENT
# 9 Writers' Rules for Writing

It's always fun to get a lagniappe. That's what my friends in New Orleans call a small surprise gift that a merchant adds to a customer's purchase (think "baker's dozen" = 13). With that in mind, for those of you who were clever enough to look beyond the body of this book or among those who habitually start at the back of reading material, here's a lagniappe: rules of writing from David Ogilvy, Neil Gaiman, Henry Miller, Jeanette Winterson, Mark Twain, William Faulkner, Zadie Smith, C. S. Lewis, and George Orwell.

## David Ogilvy – 10 Tips on Writing

The better you write, the higher you go in Ogilvy & Mather. People who think well, write well.

Woolly minded people write woolly memos, woolly letters and woolly speeches.

Good writing is not a natural gift. You have to learn to write well. Here are 10 hints:

1. Read the Roman-Raphaelson book on writing. Read it three times.
2. Write the way you talk. Naturally.
3. Use short words, short sentences and short paragraphs.
4. Never use jargon words like *reconceptualize, demassification, attitudinally, judgmentally*. They are hallmarks of a pretentious ass.
5. Never write more than two pages on any subject.
6. Check your quotations.
7. Never send a letter or a memo on the day you write it. Read it aloud the next morning — and then edit it.
8. If it is something important, get a colleague to improve it.
9. Before you send your letter or your memo, make sure it is crystal clear what you want the recipient to do.
10. If you want ACTION, don't write. Go and tell the guy what you want.

## Neil Gaiman – 8 Rules of Writing

1. Write

2. Put one word after another. Find the right word, put it down.

3. Finish what you're writing. Whatever you have to do to finish it, finish it.

4. Put it aside. Read it pretending you've never read it before. Show it to friends whose opinion you respect and who like the kind of thing that this is.

5. Remember: when people tell you something's wrong or doesn't work for them, they are almost always right. When they tell you exactly what they think is wrong and how to fix it, they are almost always wrong.

6. Fix it. Remember that, sooner or later, before it ever reaches perfection, you will have to let it go and move on and start to write the next thing. Perfection is like chasing the horizon. Keep moving.

7. Laugh at your own jokes.

8. The main rule of writing is that if you do it with enough assurance and confidence, you're allowed to do whatever you like. (That may be a rule for life as well as for writing. But it's definitely true for writing.) So write your story as it needs to be written. Write it honestly, and tell it as best you can. I'm not sure that there are any other rules. Not ones that matter.

## Henry Miller – 11 Commandments of Writing

1. Work on one thing at a time until finished.

2. Start no more new books, add no more new material to 'Black Spring.'

3. Don't be nervous. Work calmly, joyously, recklessly on whatever is in hand.

4. Work according to Program and not according to mood. Stop at the appointed time!

5. When you can't create you can work.

6. Cement a little every day, rather than add new fertilizers.

7. Keep human! See people, go places, drink if you feel like it.

8. Don't be a draught-horse! Work with pleasure only.

9. Discard the Program when you feel like it—but go back to it next day. Concentrate. Narrow down. Exclude.

10. Forget the books you want to write. Think only of the book you are writing.

11. Write first and always. Painting, music, friends, cinema, all these come afterwards.

## Jeanette Winterson – 10 Rules of Writing

1. Turn up for work. Discipline allows creative freedom. No discipline equals no freedom.

2. Never stop when you are stuck. You may not be able to solve the problem, but turn aside and write something else. Do not stop altogether.

3. Love what you do.

4. Be honest with yourself. If you are no good, accept it. If the work you are doing is no good, accept it.

5. Don't hold on to poor work. If it was bad when it went in the drawer it will be just as bad when it comes out.

6. Take no notice of anyone you don't respect.

7. Take no notice of anyone with a gender agenda. A lot of men still think that women lack imagination of the fiery kind.

8. Be ambitious for the work and not for the reward.

9. Trust your creativity.

10. Enjoy this work!

## Mark Twain – 10 Tips for Writers

1. Get your facts first, and then you can distort them as much as you please.

2. Substitute "damn" every time you're inclined to write "very." Your editor will delete it and the writing will be just as it should be.

3. Write without pay until somebody offers to pay.

4. Anybody can have ideas–the difficulty is to express them without squandering a quire of paper on an idea that ought to be reduced to one glittering paragraph.

5. Great books are weighed and measured by their style and matter, and not the trimmings and shadings of their grammar.

6. When you catch an adjective, kill it. No, I don't mean utterly, but kill most of them – then the rest will be valuable.

7. I notice that you use plain, simple language, short words and brief sentences. That is the way to write English–it is the modern way and the best way. Stick to it; don't let fluff and flowers and verbosity creep in.

8. Don't say the old lady screamed. Bring her on and let her scream.

9. I don't give a damn for a man that can only spell a word one way.

10. The more you explain it, the more I don't understand it.

## William Faulkner – 9 Tips for Writers

1. Don't be 'a writer' but instead be writing. Being 'a writer' means being stagnant. The act of writing shows movement, activity, life. When you stop moving, you're dead.

2. The only rule I have is to quit while it's still hot. Never write yourself out. Always quit when it's going good.

3. A writer needs three things, experience, observation, and imagination—any two of which, at times any one of which—can supply the lack of the others.

4. Probably any story that can't be told in one sentence or at least one paragraph is not worth writing.

5. There is no mechanical way to get the writing done, no shortcut. The young writer would be a fool to follow a theory. Teach yourself by your own mistakes; people learn only by error.

6. In the heat of putting it down you might put down some extra words. If you rework it, and the words still ring true, leave them in.

7. You can always find time to write. Anybody who says he can't is living under false pretenses.

8. Read, read, read. Read everything—trash, classics, good and bad; see how they do it. When a carpenter learns his trade, he does so by observing. Read! You'll absorb it. Write. If it's good, you'll find out. If it's not, throw it out of the window.

9. Always dream and shoot higher than you know you can do. Don't bother just to be better than your contemporaries or predecessors. Try to be better than yourself.

## Zadie Smith – 10 Rules of Writing

1. When still a child, make sure you read a lot of books. Spend more time doing this than anything else.

2. When an adult, try to read your own work as a stranger would read it, or even better, as an enemy would.

3. Don't romanticise your 'vocation.' You can either write good sentences or you can't. There is no 'writer's lifestyle.' All that matters is what you leave on the page.

4. Avoid your weaknesses. But do this without telling yourself that the things you can't do aren't worth doing. Don't mask self-doubt with contempt.

5. Leave a decent space of time between writing something and editing it.

6. Avoid cliques, gangs, groups. The presence of a crowd won't make your writing any better than it is.

7. Work on a computer that is disconnected from the internet.

8. Protect the time and space in which you write. Keep everybody away from it, even the people who are most important to you.

9. Don't confuse honours with achievement.

10. Tell the truth through whichever veil comes to hand — but tell it. Resign yourself to the lifelong sadness that comes from never being satisfied.

## C. S. Lewis – 5 Rules for Writers

1. Always try to use the language so as to make quite clear what you mean and make sure your sentence couldn't mean anything else.

2. Always prefer the plain direct word to the long, vague one. Don't implement promises, but keep them.

3. Never use abstract nouns when concrete ones will do. If you mean "More people died" don't say "Mortality rose."

4. In writing. Don't use adjectives which merely tell us how you want us to feel about the thing you are describing. I mean, instead of telling us a thing was "terrible", describe it so that we'll be terrified. Don't say it was "delightful"; make us say "delightful" when we've read the description. You see, all those words (horrifying, wonderful, hideous, exquisite) are only like saying to your readers, "Please will you do my job for me."

5. Don't use words too big for the subject. Don't say "infinitely" when you mean "very"; otherwise you'll have no word left when you want to talk about something really infinite.

## George Orwell – 6 Rules for Writers

1. Never use a metaphor, simile, or other figure of speech which you are used to seeing in print.

2. Never use a long word where a short one will do.

3. If it is possible to cut a word out, always cut it out.

4. Never use the passive where you can use the active.

5. Never use a foreign phrase, a scientific word, or a jargon word if you can think of an everyday English equivalent.

6. Break any of these rules sooner than say anything outright barbarous.

## Instant Inspiration for Copywriters

1st Edition

536 Quotes by 303 People

Cover by R. Scott Frothingham

Nib Logo by Cooter Brown

Frothingham photo by DavePughDesign.com

Published by FastForward Publishing

Contact Scott Frothingham through
FastForwardResults.com
You can also find him on LinkedIn:
www.linkedin.com/in/scottfrothingham

Made in the USA
Las Vegas, NV
21 November 2022

59931841R00072